FAVORITE Hymns AT THE PIANO

ARRANGED BY
WILLIAM GILLOCK

ISBN 978-1-4584-0303-2

EXCLUSIVELY DISTRIBUTED BY

WILLIS MUSIC

HAL•LEONARD®
CORPORATION
7777 W. BLUEMOUND RD. P.O. BOX 13819
MILWAUKEE, WISCONSIN 53213

Visit Hal Leonard Online at
www.halleonard.com

Contents

Gloria Patri

CHARLES MEINEKE, 1782 - 1850

Glo-ry be to the Fa-ther, and to the Son, and to the Ho - ly Ghost; As it was in the be-gin-ning, is now and al-ways shall be, world. with-out end, A - men, A - men.

Doxology

From PSALM C

Melody from GENEVA PSALTER, 1557

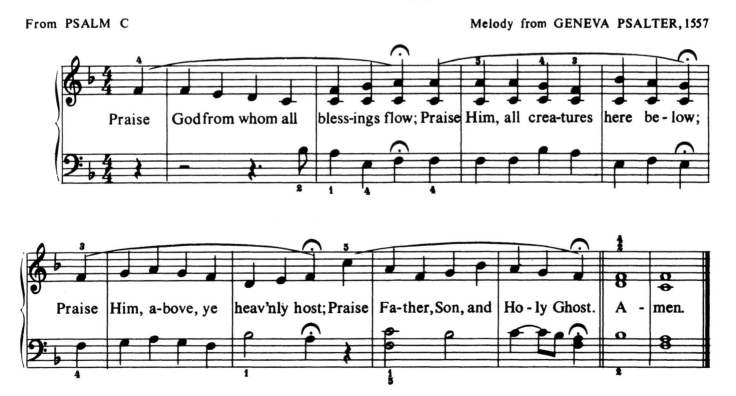

Praise God from whom all bless-ings flow; Praise Him, all crea-tures here be-low; Praise Him, a-bove, ye heav'nly host; Praise Fa-ther, Son, and Ho - ly Ghost. A - men.

4

Holy, Holy, Holy

REGINALD HEBER, 1783 - 1826

JOHN B. DYKES, 1823 - 1876

Ho - ly, ho - ly, ho - ly! Lord God Al - might - y!

Ear - ly in the morn - ing our song shall rise to Thee;

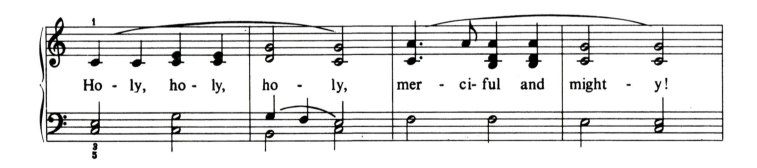

Ho - ly, ho - ly, ho - ly, mer - ci - ful and might - y!

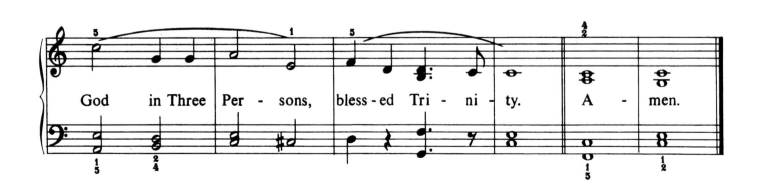

God in Three Per - sons, bless - ed Tri - ni - ty. A - men.

My Faith Looks Up to Thee

RAY PALMER, 1808 - 1887

LOWELL MASON , 1792 - 1872

My faith looks up to Thee, Thou lamb of Cal - va - ry,

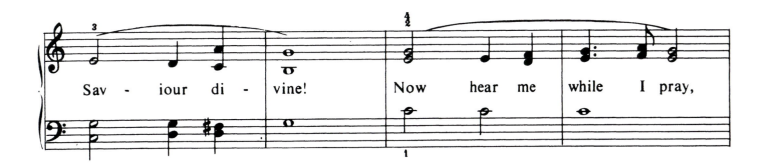

Sav - iour di - vine! Now hear me while I pray,

Take all my guilt a - way, Oh, let me from this day be

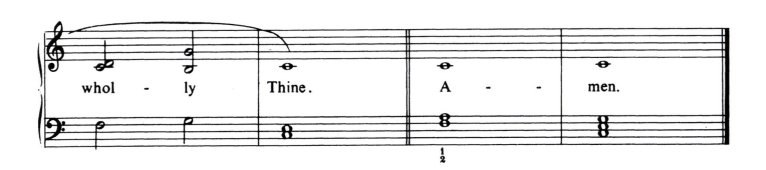

whol - ly Thine. A - men.

Sun of My Soul

JOHN KEBEL, 1792-1866

From KATHOLISCHES GESANGBUCH, 1774

Sun of my soul,_____ Thou Sav - iour dear,

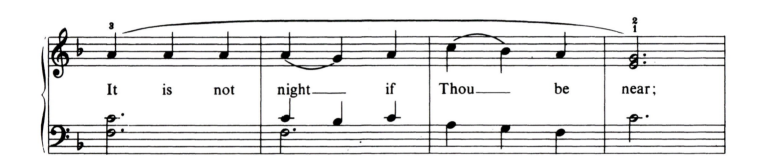

It is not night_____ if Thou_____ be near;

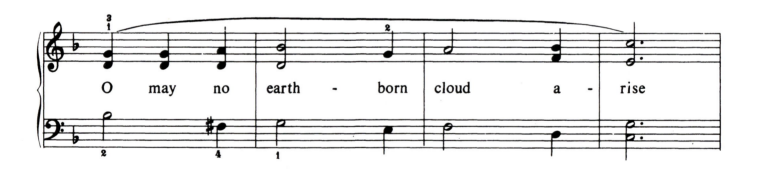

O may no earth - born cloud a - rise

To hide Thee from Thy ser - vant's eyes. A - men.

Come, Thou Almighty King

ANONYMOUS

FELICE DE GIARDINI, 1716-1796

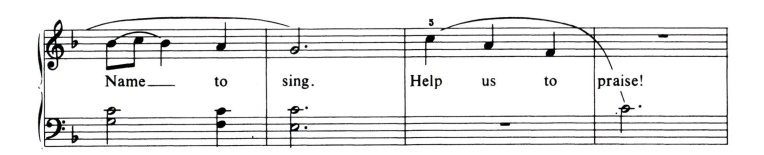

Come, thou al - might - y King. Help us Thy

Name___ to sing. Help us to praise!

Fa - ther all glo - ri - ous, O'er all vic - to - ri - ous,

Come and reign o - ver us, An - cient of Days! A - men.

Onward, Christian Soldiers

SABINE BARING-GOULD, 1834-1924   ARTHUR S. SULLIVAN, 1842-1900

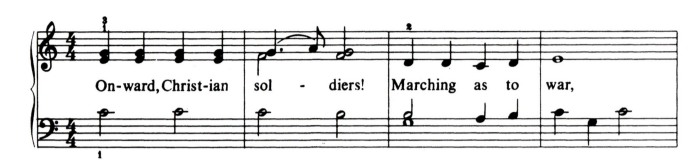

On-ward, Christ-ian sol - diers! Marching as to war,

With the cross of Je - sus go - ing on be - fore.

Christ, the roy - al Mas - ter, Leads a - gainst the foe;

For-ward in - to bat - tle,___ See His ban - ners go!___

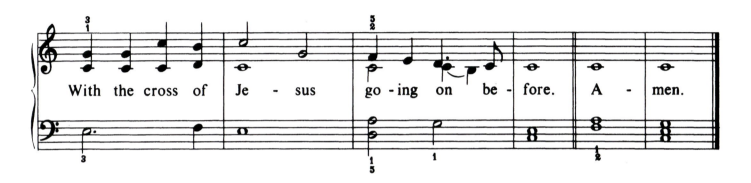

Now the Day Is Over

SABINE BARING-GOULD, 1834-1924   JOSEPH BARNBY, 1838-1896

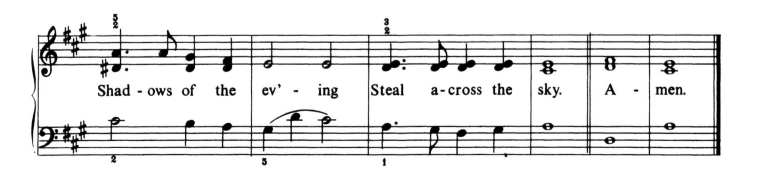

All Through the Night

H. BOULTON

WELSH FOLK MELODY

Sleep, my child, and peace at-tend thee All through the night.

Guar - dian an - gels God will send thee All through the night.

Soft the drow - sy hours are creep-ing, Hill and vale in slum - ber steep-ing,

I, my lov - ing vig - il keep-ing All through the night. A - men.

Sicilian Mariner's Hymn

JOHN FAWCETT, 1740-1817

SICILIAN FOLK MELODY

To Father, Son and Holy Ghost

ISAAC WATTS, 1674-1748

From GENEVA PSALTER, 1551

O Come, Immanuel

12th Century Latin
Tr. by JOHN M. NEALE, 1818-1866

13th Century Plain Song

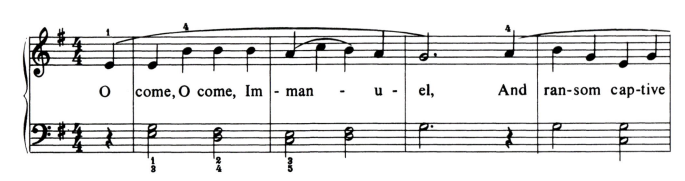

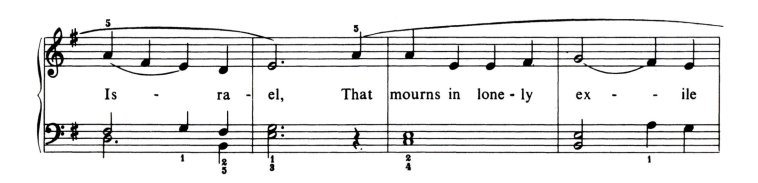

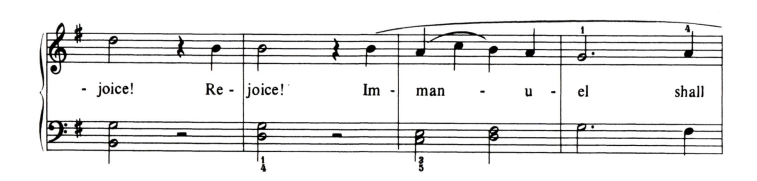

come to thee, O Is - - ra - el! A - men.

For the Beauty of the Earth

FOLLIOT S. PIERPONT, 1835-1917

CONRAD KOCHER, 1786-1872

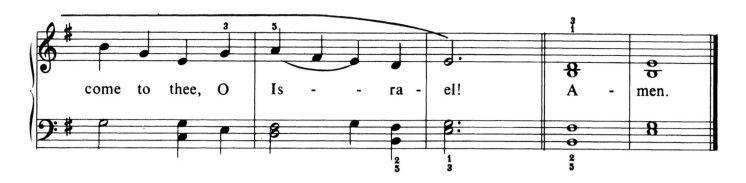

For the_ beau - ty of the earth, For the glo - ry of the skies,

For the_ love which from our birth O - ver and a - round us lies:

Lord of all, to Thee we raise This our hymn of grate-ful praise. A - men.

We Gather Together

Anonymous
Tr. by THEODORE BAKER

NETHERLAND FOLK MELODY, 1625

We gath - er to - geth - er to ask the Lord's bless - ing; He

chast - ens and hast - ens His will to make known; The wick - ed op -

press - ing now cease___ from de - press - ing, Sing prais - es to His

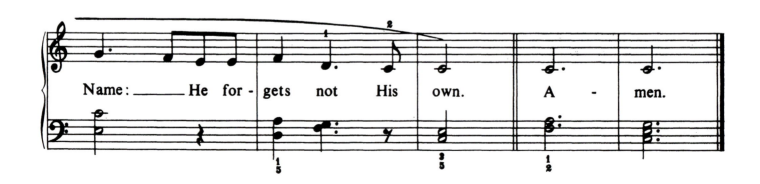

Name: ___ He for - gets not His own. A - men.

Fairest Lord Jesus

17th Century German
Translator unknown

SILESIAN FOLK MELODY
From Schlesische Volkslieder, 1842

Fair - est Lord Je - sus, Rul - er of all na - ture,

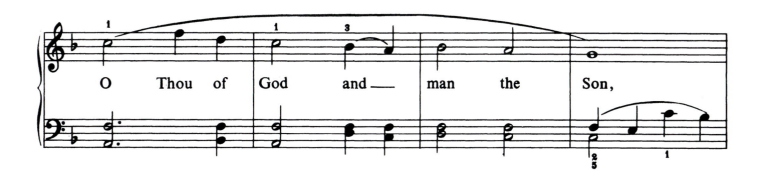

O Thou of God and — man the Son,

Thee will I cher - ish, Thee will I hon - or, Thee,

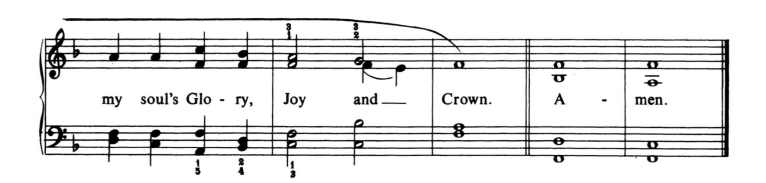

my soul's Glo - ry, Joy and — Crown. A - men.

From All that Dwell Below the Skies

From PSALM CXVII
Isaac Watts, 1674 - 1748

From GEISTLICHE KIRKENGESANG, 1623

From all that dwell be-low the skies Let the Cre-a-tor's praise a - rise:

Al-le - lu - ia; Al-le - lu - ia! Let the Re-deem-er's name be sung

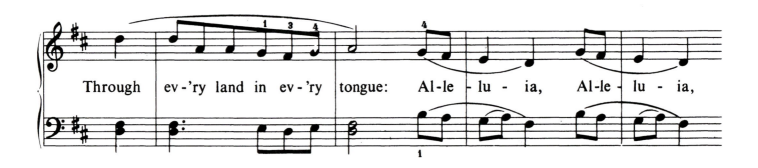

Through ev-'ry land in ev-'ry tongue: Al-le - lu - ia, Al-le - lu - ia,

Al-le - lu - ia, Al-le - lu - ia, Al-le - lu - ia! A - men.

Come, Ye Thankful People

HENRY ALFORD, 1810-1871   GEORGE J. ELVEY, 1816-1893

Come, ye thank-ful peo - ple, come, Raise the song of har-vest-home

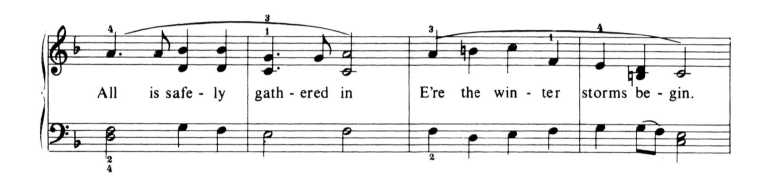

All is safe - ly gath - ered in E're the win - ter storms be - gin.

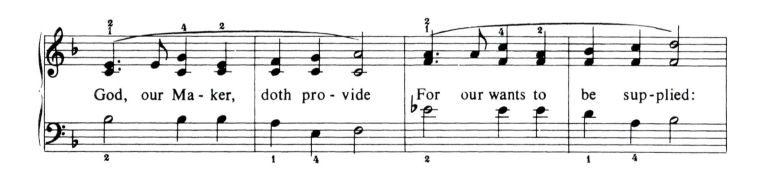

God, our Ma - ker, doth pro - vide For our wants to be sup-plied:

Come to God's own tem-ple, come, Raise the song of har-vest-home. A - men.

God of Our Fathers

DANIEL C. ROBERTS, 1841-1907

GEORGE W. WARREN, 1828-1902

(Trumpets) God of our fa - thers,

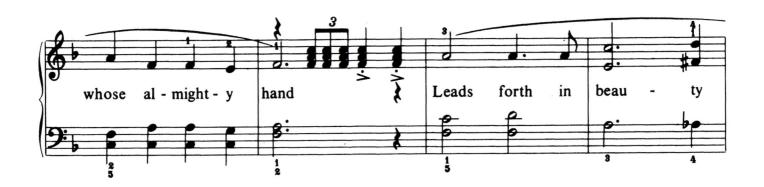

whose al - might - y hand Leads forth in beau - ty

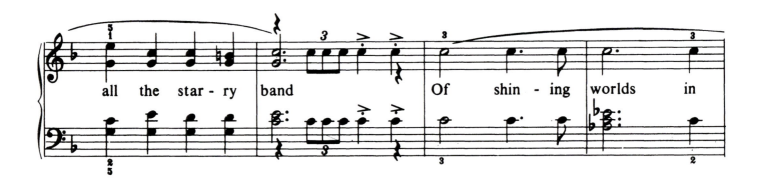

all the star - ry band Of shin - ing worlds in

splen- dor through the skies, Our grate - ful songs be -

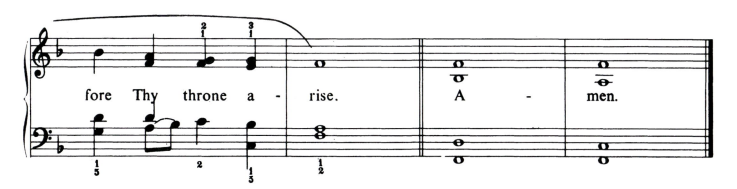

Praise, My Soul, the King of Heaven

From PSALM CIII
HENRY F. LYTE, 1793 - 1847

HENRY SMART, 1813 - 1879

The God of Abraham

DANIEL BEN JUDAH, 14th Century

HEBREW MELODY

The God of Abra-ham praise, All prais-ed be His Name,

Who was, and is, and is to be, and still the___ same!

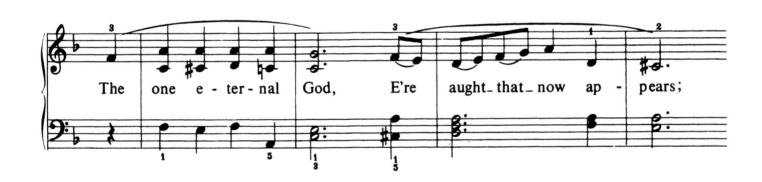

The one e - ter - nal God, E're aught_ that_ now ap - pears;

The First, the Last: be -yond all_ thought His time - less years! A - men.

Softly Now the Light of Day

GEORGE W. DOANE, 1799-1859   LOUIS MOREAU GOTTSCHALK, 1829-1869

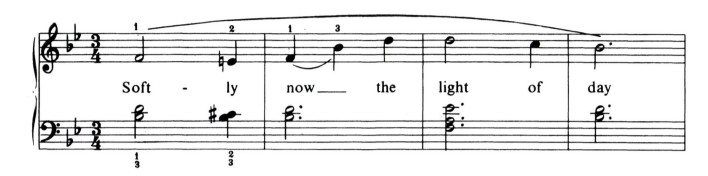

Soft - ly now the light of day

Fades up on our sights a - way; Free from

care and la - bor free, Lord we would com-

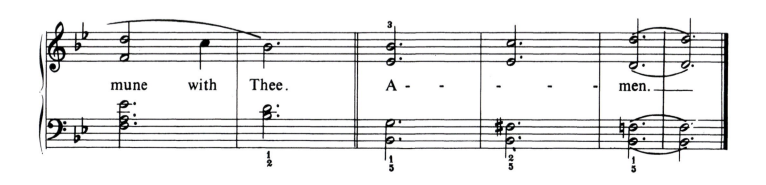

mune with Thee. A - men.

The Spacious Firmament on High

JOSEPH ADDISON, 1672 - 1719

From "THE CREATION"
FRANZ JOSEPH HAYDN, 1732 - 1809

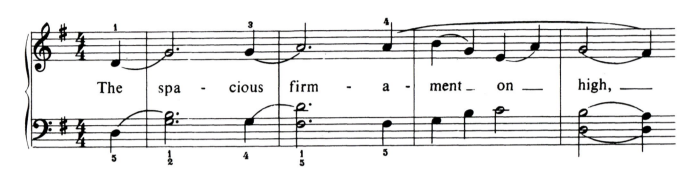

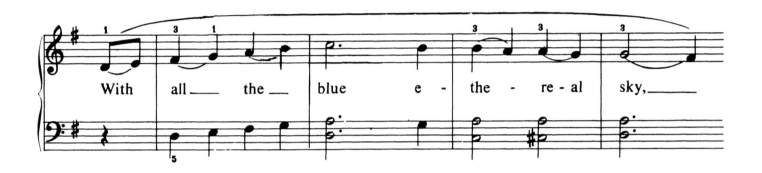

The spa - cious firm - a - ment on high,

With all the blue e - the - re - al sky,

And spang - led heav'ns, a shin - ing frame,

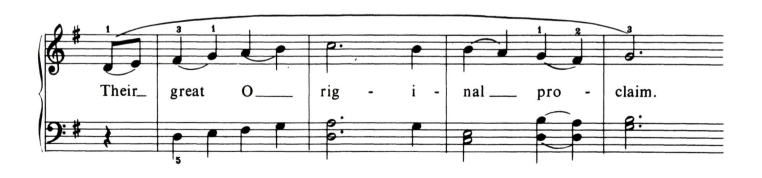

Their great O - rig - i - nal pro - claim.

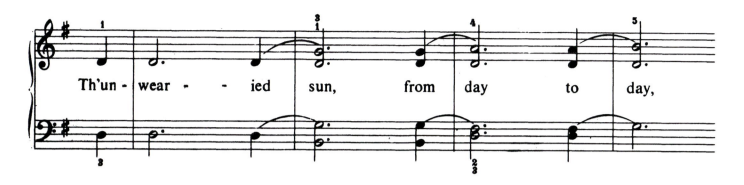

Th'un - wear - - ied sun, from day to day,

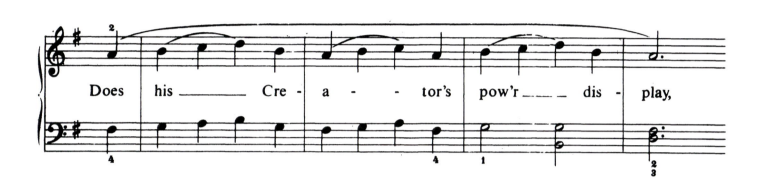

Does his ____ Cre - a - - tor's pow'r ____ dis - play,

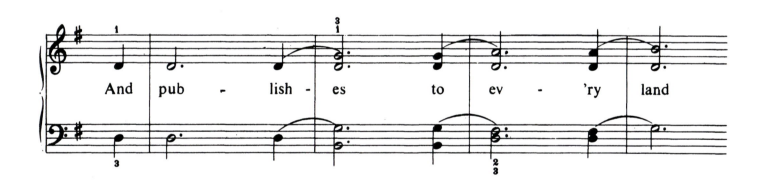

And pub - lish - es to ev - 'ry land

The work ___ of an ___ al - might - y hand. A - men.

God the Omnipotent

HENRY F. CHORLEY, 1808-1872

ALEXIS F. LVOV, 1799-1871

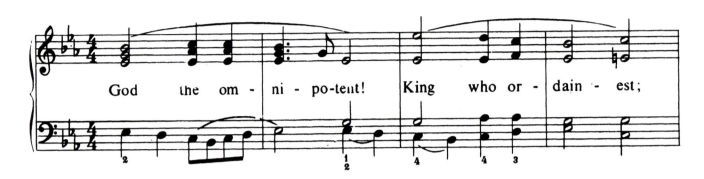

God the om - ni - po-tent! King who or - dain - est;

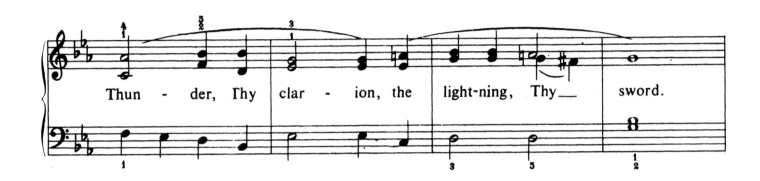

Thun - der, Thy clar - ion, the light-ning, Thy sword.

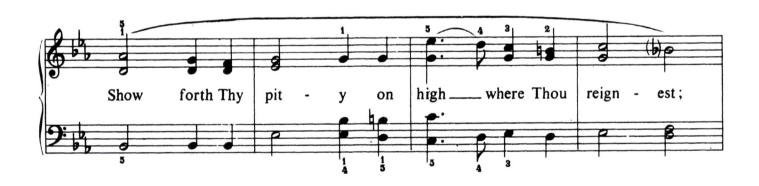

Show forth Thy pit - y on high where Thou reign - est;

Give to us peace in our time, O Lord. A - men.